Elijah Hears God Whisper

Written by Bek and Barb

Illustrated by Bill Dickson

Elijah, God's prophet, was tired and scared.

Queen Jezebel had killed many of God's prophets. Now she wanted to kill Elijah, too.

Elijah ran for his life. He escaped to the mountains and hid in the mouth of a cave.

God knew Elijah was scared. "What are you doing here?" God asked.

"I have been your faithful servant, even though all of Israel worships other gods," Elijah cried. "And now they want to kill me!"

"Go out and stand on the mountain," God told Elijah. "I will show myself to you."

A mighty wind ripped across the mountain. It tore up trees and smashed giant rocks to bits.

But God was not in the wind.

Next, a powerful earthquake shook the land. Elijah trembled.

But God was not in the earthquake.

Then a roaring fire appeared to Elijah. It burned everything in its path.

But God was not in the fire.

After the fire burned out, Elijah heard a gentle whisper.

That was God.

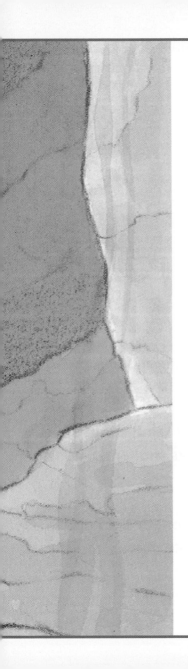

God had shown Elijah his great power. This was God's way of showing Elijah that he could protect him.

"Now go and do my work, Elijah," God said, "because I am with you."

Elijah Hears God Whisper

Life Issue: I want my child to know that God is powerful enough to protect us.

Spiritual Building Block: Confidence in God

Do the following activities to help your child understand God's power:

Sight: Look for pictures of hurricanes, earthquakes, and fires on the Internet or in an encyclopedia. Discuss with your child how God is even more powerful than these things.

Sound: Ask your child to close his eyes as you read aloud the story of Elijah in the cave from 1 Kings 19:11-13. Encourage your child to make the sounds of rocks shattering in the wind, an earthquake, a roaring fire, and a gentle whisper.

Touch: Have you child hold his arms over his head. When he can no longer hold up his arms, read 2 Corinthians 12:9 and discuss how God is strong when we are weak.

The Little Girl Lives

Written by Bek and Barb

Illustrated by Alastair Graham

Faith Kidz® is an imprint of
Cook Communications Ministries, Colorado Springs, CO 80918
Cook Communications, Paris, Ontario
Kingsway Communications, Eastbourne, England

THE LITTLE GIRL LIVES
© 2006 by Cook Communications Ministries for text and illustrations

Cover: Sandy Flewelling
Interior Design: Sandy Flewelling
Interior Layout: Julie Brangers

First Printing, 2006
Printed in India
1 2 3 4 5 6 7 8 9 10 Printing/Year 10 09 08 07 06

ISBN: 0-7814-469-1

The Little Girl Lives

My wife and I were so sad. Our daughter was sick. She was so sick we were afraid she would die.

I loved my daughter so much, I would do anything to save her life, but nothing we had tried worked. I had heard Jesus could heal people. He had just arrived in town, so I ran to find him.

When I saw Jesus, I pushed my way into the crowd and fell at his feet.

"Jesus," I cried, "my daughter is dying. Please! Come and put your hands on her. I know you can heal her so she will live."

Jesus agreed to go with me. We turned to leave, but a man stopped us. He had just come from my house. "I'm sorry," he said. "Your daughter is dead. Let's not bother the teacher anymore."

No! We were too late. I couldn't hold my sadness in any longer; I started to cry. If only we had gotten there in time.

But Jesus put his hand on my shoulder. He looked at me and said, "Don't be afraid, Jairus. Just believe and your daughter will be healed."

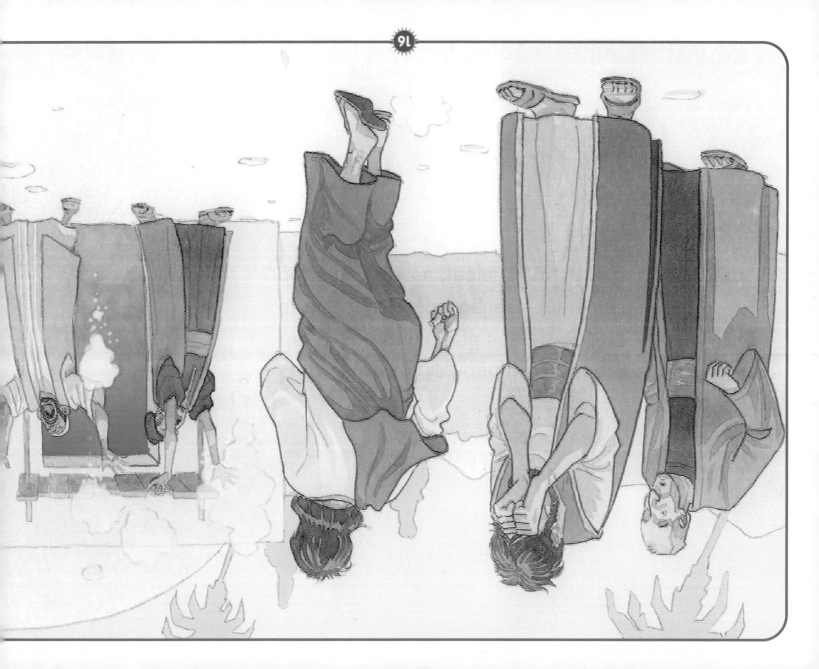

When we got to my house, there were people crying and wailing everywhere. They had heard the news that my daughter had died.

Jesus said, "What's going on here? Why is everyone so upset? The little girl isn't dead. She's only asleep."

The people at my home were shocked. Some of them laughed at Jesus; others got angry. How could Jesus say such a thing?

My wife was in the house with our daughter. Jesus brought his disciples and me into the room where she lay, and closed the door.

Then he took my daughter by the hand and said, "My child, get up."

As soon as Jesus spoke, my daughter opened her eyes.

What a miracle! Jesus had healed my daughter.

My little girl got up and walked around. She even ate some food! We were all amazed.

I was so thankful to
have my little girl back.

Faith Parenting Guide

Ages 4-7

Faith

The Little Girl Lives

Life Issue: I want my child to realize that God will do what he promises to do.

Spiritual Building Block: Faith

Do the following activities to help your child have faith in God:

Sight: Read Genesis 9:8-17. Talk about how God has kept this promise. Find a picture of a rainbow in a book or on the Internet. Have your child copy the picture and hang it in his or her room as a reminder that God keeps his promises.

Sound: Talk about a time that God answered a prayer.

Touch: Ask your child to copy this Bible verse from Acts 27:25: "…for I have faith."

Words on a Wall

Written by Bek and Barb

Illustrated by Elizabeth Swisher

The king of Babylon was happy. A thousand people were partying at a feast in his palace. "Cheers!" King Belshazzar said, lifting a golden cup stolen from God's temple. "Cheers!" everyone cried as they drank and praised the false gods of Babylon.

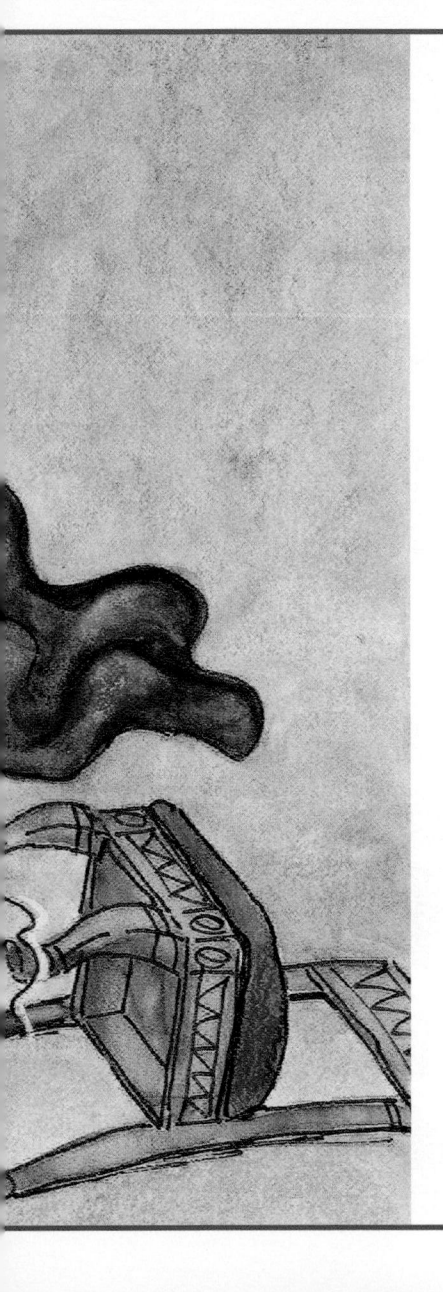

Suddenly, the king turned pale. "What is that?" he cried, pointing to the wall.

A floating hand was writing strange words on the palace wall.

Everyone panicked. The king was so frightened, he could barely stand up. "What could it mean?" he asked.

No one could tell the king what the mysterious words meant.

"I know," said the king's mother. "Bring us Daniel. He will be able to read the writing on the wall."

"**D**aniel!" the king said. "You've got to help me. Can you solve the riddle of these words?"

"Yes, I can," Daniel said. "But you won't like what I have to say. You have not honored God. You drank wine out of cups stolen from God's temple. You worshipped false gods. This is God's way of saying that you are not a good leader. You will no longer rule over Babylon, and this kingdom will be given to someone else."

The room fell silent and the king's party ended. That same night, God's words about King Belshazzar came true.

Words on a Wall

Life Issue: I want my child to honor God.

Spiritual Building Block: Worship

Do the following activities to help your child learn how to worship God:

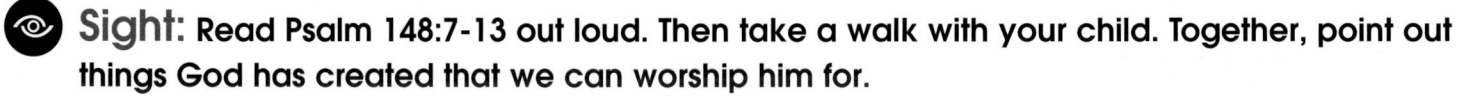

Sight: Read Psalm 148:7-13 out loud. Then take a walk with your child. Together, point out things God has created that we can worship him for.

Sound: Sing your child's favorite worship song with him or her.

Touch: Make a list with your child of things we can worship God for. Spend a few minutes praying with your child.